b

Oxford**basics**

Simple Writing Activities

JILL HADFIELD
CHARLES HADFIELD

OXFORD
UNIVERSITY PRESS

OXFORD
UNIVERSITY PRESS

Great Clarendon Street, Oxford OX2 6DP

Oxford University Press is a department of the University
of Oxford. It furthers the University's objective of excellence
in research, scholarship, and education by publishing
worldwide in

Oxford New York

Athens Auckland Bangkok Bogotá Buenos Aires
Calcutta Cape Town Chennai Dar es Salaam Delhi
Florence Hong Kong Istanbul Karachi Kuala Lumpur
Madrid Melbourne Mexico City Mumbai Nairobi Paris
São Paulo Singapore Taipei Tokyo Toronto Warsaw

with associated companies in Berlin Ibadan

OXFORD and OXFORD ENGLISH are registered trade marks of
Oxford University Press in the UK and in certain other countries

Illustrations by Margaret Welbank

ISBN 0 19 442170 8

Printed in China

Contents

Foreword

There is a formidable range of materials published worldwide for teachers of English as a Foreign Language. However, many of these materials, especially those published in English-speaking countries, assume that teachers using them will be working with smallish classes and have abundant resources available to them. Also many, if not most, of these materials make implicit culturally-biased assumptions about the beliefs and values of the teachers and learners.

This situation is ironic in view of the fact that the vast majority of English as a Foreign Language classrooms do not correspond at all to these conditions. Typically, classes are large, resources are limited, and teachers have very few opportunities for training and professional development. Also, the cultural assumptions of teachers and learners in many parts of the world may vary quite significantly from those of materials writers and publishers.

This book is an attempt to address this situation. The authors present thirty lessons at elementary level, each with the same methodological framework. The lessons are explained in clear, accessible language, and none of them require sophisticated resources. Instead, they call on the basic human resources which all teachers and learners bring with them to class. The language points covered are ones found in a typical elementary course, and the topics are those which form part of everybody's daily lives, for example, families, homes, and leisure activities.

Most importantly, however, the book offers a framework for teachers who lack training and support. The hope and the expectation is that such teachers will begin by following each step of a lesson quite closely, but, as their confidence increases, will adapt and add to the techniques presented here, responding to the particular needs and abilities of their learners.

This is an important book: one of the few attempts to address the problems of the 'silent majority' of teachers worldwide who have little or no training, and few resources to work with.

ALAN MALEY
Assumption University
Bangkok, Thailand

Introduction

English is taught all over the world, by all sorts of teachers to all sorts of learners. Schools and classrooms vary enormously in their wealth and their provision of equipment. Learners are very different from place to place. But, whatever the conditions in which you are working, there is one resource which is universal and unlimited: the human mind and imagination. This is probably the single most valuable teaching and learning resource we have. Nothing can replace it. In even the most 'hi-tech' environment, a lack of imagination and humanity will make the most up-to-date and sophisticated resources seem dull; conversely, the most simple resources can be the most exciting and useful.

We have been fortunate to spend quite a lot of our time working not only in hi-tech environments with computers and video, but also in classrooms where there is little more than blackboard and chalk and some out-of-date coursebooks. Some of our most interesting learning and teaching experiences (as Confucius said, a teacher is 'always ready to teach; always ready to learn') have been not in the comfortable well-resourced small classrooms of a private language school, but in classrooms where only the minimum of equipment has been available. Equally, some of our most memorable teaching experiences in 'hi-tech' classrooms have been when we have abandoned the cassette or video or glossy coursebook and got to work with that most precious resource of all, the learners' own experience and imagination.

Teachers often have to use materials which are out of date, or contain subject-matter irrelevant to their particular group of learners. For example, we have had great difficulty explaining the concepts of the fridge-freezer and microwave oven to Tibetans. In the same way, learners who have spent all their lives in northern countries might have difficulty with an exercise from an African textbook which asks if they prefer yam or cassava. So over the last few years we have been trying to design materials which can be used in as wide a range of teaching situations as possible.

The activities we suggest are as flexible as the human imagination is creative; they are 'teacher resource material' which teachers will be able to adjust to suit their particular environment. In thinking about universally applicable, 'lo-tech' materials we have come up with a list of criteria that need to be met. The materials will need to:

- be usable in large classes as well as small.
- be suitable for adult learners as well as secondary learners, and if possible easily adaptable to a primary context.
- be centred on the universals of human experience.
- cover the main language skills and have a useful base of grammar and topic vocabulary.

- be traditional enough to be recognizable to all teachers, and thus give them a sense of security, while providing communicative activities for learners.
- be non-threatening in the demands they make on learners.
- be teacher-based 'resource material' rather than books for learners.
- assume that no technical and reprographic resources are available, and be based on the human resource rather than the technical.
- be culturally neutral, not context-bound, and thus flexible and easily adaptable by the teachers to their own culture and teaching context.
- be flexible enough to complement a standard syllabus or coursebook.

Simple Writing Activities

This book contains thirty activities, designed according to the criteria above, for developing the writing skill at elementary level. Each activity has three main stages:

- **Lead-in**—This introduces the learners to the topic, and focuses their attention.
- **Organizing texts**—This stage provides controlled writing practice in preparation for a freer writing task.
- **Creating texts**—This stage gives the learners the opportunity to use the knowledge they have acquired in the previous two stages in producing their own text. The teacher provides a context and a reason for writing.

Lead-in

Writing is easier if the learners are prepared for the task, and if their imaginations are stimulated beforehand. The purpose of the lead-in is to 'warm up' the learners, in other words, to start them thinking about the topic and practising some of the language that will be needed when they actually come to write.

Organizing texts

The aim of this stage is to give the learners controlled writing practice before they attempt a freer writing task. This is important because the language of writing is different from that of speech. In speech, utterances tend to be short or incomplete, and the language used is often colloquial, and may break grammatical rules. However, most written language is more formal and elaborate, and follows certain conventions.

The text organization techniques used in this book are as follows:

- **Completion**—The learners fill in the blanks in a text or a crossword puzzle with an appropriate word or phrase. This technique can give learners practice in a particular language point, for example, place prepositions.
- **Describing a picture**—The learners write a description of a picture. They may then discuss the best order in which to describe the different elements which go to make up the picture. This gives them practice in organizing a spatial description.
- **Joining**—Learners join words or sentences using a linking word, such as 'and' or 'but'. This technique helps learners to develop the skill of linking ideas logically and writing more fluently.
- **Matching**—The learners have to match the two separate halves of sentences which are written in the form of two lists. This technique helps learners to understand how sentences are constructed and which words can go with other words.
- **Reordering**—Sentences or texts are given to the learners in muddled order and they have to rearrange them in the correct order. Reordering sentences is useful for teaching word order, while reordering texts helps learners practise choosing a logical sequence for sentences.
- **Substitution**—In this technique a basic sentence framework is written on the board. The learner can vary this by choosing different words or phrases at certain points. This shows learners how a basic sentence form may be used with slight variations to express a number of different meanings.
- **Writing from notes**—The learners are given notes to expand into text. This gives them practice in arranging their ideas coherently.

Creating texts

It is difficult to write when you don't know who you are writing to, or why. In real life we always have a reason for writing: for example, to answer a letter, prepare a shopping list, or make notes for a talk. In the classroom there is often no apparent reason for writing beyond 'The teacher said do this for homework'. If, however, you provide the learners with a context for creating a written text, you can make the task much more concrete and interesting. There is a wide variety of techniques which you can use. The ones we have used in this book are as follows:

- **Writing from a picture**—The learners use a picture as a starting-off point for creating a text.
- **Responding to a text**—The learners are given a text to read before they write, for example a poem or a letter. The text acts as a source of inspiration, and useful words and phrases which they can use in their own writing. Alternatively, they may be asked to use their

own texts from the 'Creating texts' part of the lesson.

- ■ **Survey and report**—In this technique the writing task is preceded by a speaking task in which the learners have to gather information from each other and use it to write a report. This gives them something concrete to write about, and a definite purpose in writing.
- ■ **Visualization**—The learners close their eyes and visualize a scene which you describe to them. They then write about the scene they have imagined. They may share what they have written with another learner.

Learners can also act as each other's audience. This is the most immediate and direct way of providing the writer with a reader. There are various techniques which can be used:

- ■ **Write and do**—The learners write texts, for example, a letter, a series of instructions, or a description of a scene. Other learners read them and respond in an appropriate way, for example by creating a tableau of the scene.
- ■ **Write and draw**—The learners draw a picture and write a description of it. They either pass their description to another learner who has to draw a picture of it, or the pictures and descriptions are put up in the classroom and the learners match them.
- ■ **Write and guess**—The learners write a description or riddle for others to read and guess the person or object being described.

Teachers often set writing for homework, and some of the activities in this book may be given for homework if time is short. However, they are really designed to be done in class, so that you can circulate while the learners are working, supply any vocabulary they need, and correct or explain any mistakes as they arise. It is also an advantage for learners to receive immediate feedback from one another on their writing.

. . . .

Materials

A wide variety of text types is used in this book. These include descriptions, narratives, reports, instructions, lists, poems, and letters. This helps to provide interest and equips the learners to deal more effectively with different kinds of writing.

Many activities suggest the use of a poster. This is simply a text written out in large letters, or a picture, on a big sheet of paper. If you prepare posters before the lesson, it means that you do not have the time-consuming task of writing or drawing on the board while the lesson is in progress. This is a particular advantage if you are not very confident about your drawing skills. It also means that you will not have to write out the text, or draw the picture, again the next time you want to use it.

If you decide to use posters, try to find a cheap source of sheets of paper. In Madagascar, for example, the teachers we worked with found the sheets of paper used for wrapping vegetables in the market were ideal for making posters. A good way to fix posters to the board is to pin a length of string along the top of the board like a clothes-line. You can then use clothes-pegs to pin your posters to the string!

An alternative to drawings on posters is drawings on smaller pieces of card (but still large enough for all the learners to see). These are usually known as 'flashcards'. They are used in 11 'Colours' and 24 'Daily routines'.

Correction

After some of the activities you will want to correct the learners' work in order to give them feedback about their progress. It can be very discouraging for learners if their work comes back covered in red ink, and this can have a destructive effect on their creativity, enthusiasm, and confidence. In addition, if every mistake is corrected by the teacher, this robs the learner of a valuable learning experience—how to spot and correct their own mistakes. You can reduce the 'big red pen' effect, and help learners to self-correct by using the following strategies:

- Working with learners as they are writing, supplying vocabulary and pointing out mistakes.
- Getting learners to work together or read each other's work and help each other with mistakes.
- When you correct learners' work, use symbols in the margin to indicate that there is a mistake in that line rather than correcting the mistake yourself. It is then up to the learner to work out what was wrong, and what the correct version should be. Useful symbols are:

*	well done
O	organization
Sp	spelling
T	tense
Pr	preposition
WO	word order

A   article

Ag agreement (singular/plural, etc.)

P   punctuation

V   vocabulary

Gr other grammar mistake

You may not want to correct every mistake in a learner's work, but prefer to concentrate on one specific area at a time, for example, tenses, spelling, or prepositions. If you adopt this system you will need to give learners a little time after you hand back their writing tasks to work out what was wrong, write in the correct version, and ask you for help if they still do not understand. If most of the class made the same or similar mistakes, you may want to devote a lesson or part of a lesson to remedial work on this area.

Building a lesson

There are four companion books to this one, *Presenting New Language, Simple Listening Activities, Simple Speaking Activities,* and *Simple Reading Activities.* All of these also contain thirty activities, and in all five books the topics and the language presented and practised correspond. So, for example, activity 1 in all five books is about 'Greetings and introductions' and activity 30 is about 'Describing actions'. The activities in each book are graded, following a basic structural syllabus. This means that you can design your own lesson or sequence of lessons using material from any, or all, of the books, depending on your learners' needs and the time available.

Activities

1 Greetings and introductions

LANGUAGE	**Hello. My name's _____.** **What's your name?** **Nice to meet you.**
TECHNIQUES	Organizing texts: completion. Creating texts: writing from a picture.
MATERIALS	The dialogue below; the pictures below, on posters or on the board.
PREPARATION	Prepare the poster if you are using one.
TIME GUIDE	30 minutes.

Lead-in

1 Walk around the class introducing yourself to the learners. Use 'Hello. My name's _____. What's your name?'

2 Put up these pictures.

Tell the learners to repeat the dialogue. Then cover, or rub out, the names, and get the learners to repeat the dialogue again, using their own names.

Organizing texts: completion

3 Write this gapped dialogue on the board:

BEN   Hello. _____ _____ Ben. _____ your _____?

KATE My name's _____. Nice _____ meet _____.

BEN   _____ to _____ you too.

Ask the learners to copy the dialogue and fill in the gaps.

4 When everyone has finished, write in the missing words on the board and get the learners to check their work.

Creating texts: writing from a picture

5 Put up these pictures. Get the learners to copy them and to write in the dialogue.

6 Ask one or two pairs of learners to read out their sentences in the correct order, one taking Ben's part and the other Kate's (get them to use their own names if they prefer).

Comment

If appropriate, change the names to more familiar local names.

2 The alphabet

LANGUAGE	The letters of the alphabet.
TECHNIQUES	Organizing texts: reordering. Creating texts: writing from a picture.
MATERIALS	The jumbled words below; the pictures below, on a poster or on the board.
PREPARATION	Prepare the poster if you are using one.
TIME GUIDE	40 minutes.

Lead-in

1 Spell out this dialogue (i.e. pronounce each letter separately):

H – e – l – l – o.   M – y   n – a – m – e' – s   B – e – n.

W – h – a – t' – s   y – o – u – r   n – a – m – e?

M – y   n – a – m – e' – s   K – a – t – e.

N – i – c – e   t – o   m – e – e – t   y – o – u.

Tell the learners to put up their hand and tell the class when they guess a word.

Organizing texts: reordering

2 Write these jumbled words on the board:

LOLHE	CEIN
NEB	TEME
MEAN'S	OT
YM	OYU
AMNE	TEKA
UYOR	YM
S'THWA	ES'MNA

3 Divide the learners into pairs, A and B. Ask A to look at the jumbled words in the first column and to sort them out. B should do the same for the second column.

4 When they have finished, ask A to dictate his or her words to B, who should write them down. Then get B to do the same for A. Tell them to make a dialogue from the words.

Creating texts: writing from a picture

5 Put up these pictures:

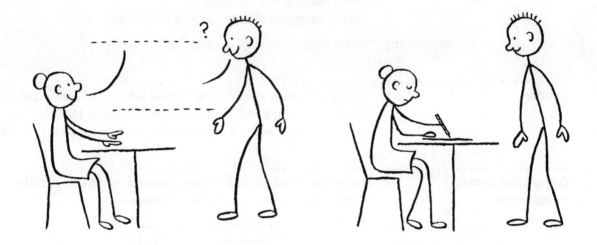

6 Tell the learners to copy the pictures and write the dialogue in the spaces.

7 Get learners to compare their dialogues with others in the class.

Comment

Learners can write their own dialogues using different names, and dictate them to one another.

3 Numbers

LANGUAGE Numbers.

TECHNIQUES Organizing texts: completion.
Creating texts: responding to a text.

MATERIALS The crossword below, a blank version with clues and a version with answers, on two posters; the poem below, on a poster or on the board; examples of the objects in the poem.

PREPARATION Adapt the poem if necessary. Make the crossword posters, and the poem poster if you are using one.
Collect examples of the objects in the poem.

TIME GUIDE 50 minutes.

Lead-in

1 Give the learners some simple 'mental arithmetic' with numbers up to 20. For example, ask them to add 6 and 4, and 18 and 2. You could make this into a competition between two teams if you like.

Organizing texts: completion

2 Put up the blank version of the crossword. Make sure that the learners understand how to fill in a crossword.

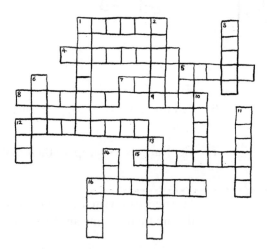

Across	Down
1 6x2	1 16-3
4 8+11	2 10+1
5 1+2	3 3+4
7 8-7	5 5x2
8 3x5	6 3+2
9 3x3	10 4x2
12 20-3	11 10x2
15 6x3	12 12-6
16 7x2	13 8x2
	14 7-5
	16 2x2

3 Tell the learners to copy the grid, but not the clues.

4 Ask them to complete the crossword on their own, and then to compare their answers in pairs.

5 Put up the version with answers.

**Creating texts:
responding to a text**

6 Put up this poem. (If necessary, change some of the objects to those your learners are more likely to have in their schoolbags.)

In Sam's schoolbag

ONE English book,
TWO wooden rulers,
THREE class notebooks,
FOUR black pens,
FIVE chocolate biscuits,
SIX paper hankies,
SEVEN pop cassettes,
EIGHT coloured pencils,
NINE bus tickets,
TEN sticky sweets.

Show the class an example of each object in the poem, and ask the learners to identify it. Tell them they may use their own language if they don't know the word in English.

7 Read the poem, holding up an example of each object as you read each line.

8 Get the class to read the poem in chorus. Then ask for a volunteer to come out and hold up each object as the rest of the class read the poem.

9 Ask the learners to tell you about other things they have in their schoolbags. Tell them they may use their own language if they don't know the word in English. Translate their suggestions into English and write them on the board.

10 Ask the learners to write a poem like 'In Sam's schoolbag', called 'In my schoolbag'.

4 Telling the time

LANGUAGE	**What time is it?**
	It's _____ o'clock.
	Numbers.
TECHNIQUES	Organizing texts: completion.
	Creating texts: responding to a text.
MATERIALS	Notes and clock faces, on posters or on the board; diary pages, on a poster or on the board.
PREPARATION	If necessary, adapt the notes to suit your learners' ages and cultures. Prepare the posters if you are using them.
TIME GUIDE	40 minutes.

Lead-in

1 Revise times by drawing a clock face on the board, drawing in the hands at different times, and asking the learners to tell you what time it is. Use:

What time is it?

It's _____ o'clock.

Organizing texts: completion

2 Put up these notes and clock faces:

Sue, see you after school at _____. Tom

Helen, meet you at the cinema at _____. James

Tom, meet me for lunch at _____. Helen

James, the meeting is at _____. Sue

14

(If necessary, teach 'see', 'school', 'meet', 'cinema', 'lunch', and 'meeting'.) Tell the learners to match the notes and the clock faces.

3   Get the learners to copy the notes and write in the times in words.

4   Check the answers with the whole class.

5   Put up these notes:

Sam, _____ you at the _____ at eight o'clock. Tom.

Tom, _____ you after _____ at four o'clock. Sue.

Sue, _____ me for _____ at twelve fifteen. Helen.

Helen, the _____ is at ten thirty. Mark.

6   Ask the learners to copy the notes and fill in the gaps with appropriate vocabulary items from the first set of notes.

7   Check the answers with the whole class.

Creating texts: responding to a text

8   Put up these diary pages:

Meet Sam. Pegasus Cinema. Film—8.15.
Meeting—3.20. Tell Tom.
Dinner with James. Huang Shan restaurant —7.30.
Arrange to see Sue after work—6.00 Casablanca Cafe.

Tell the learners to write notes to Sam, Tom, James, and Sue making these arrangements.

9   Ask some learners to read out their notes to the whole class.

5 Personal information

LANGUAGE   My name is _____.

I am _____.

I am a _____.

I am from _____.

I live at _____.

My hobbies are _____ and _____.

TECHNIQUES   Organizing texts: reordering.
Creating texts: responding to a text.

MATERIALS   Jumbled sentences; letter, on a poster or on the board.

PREPARATION   Prepare the poster if you are using one.

TIME GUIDE   40 minutes.

Lead-in

1   Ask the learners if they have, or have ever had, a penpal. Ask some questions about their penpals, for example:

What is his or her name?

Where is he or she from?

Organizing texts: reordering

2   Write these jumbled sentences on the board:

name my John is.

live I at 79 Abbey Road

Senegal from I am

learner a I'm

15 I am

hobbies are my dancing swimming and

Tell the learners to write them out correctly. Remind them that each sentence should begin with a capital letter and end with a full stop. When they have finished, get them to compare their answers in pairs.

3   Ask individual learners to read out their answers to the whole class.

**Creating texts:
responding to a text**

4 Put up this letter:

> Dear penpal,
>
> Let me introduce myself.
>
> I'm 21 years old.
>
> My name's Sanjay Jhabvala.
>
> I'm from India.
>
> I'm a postman.
>
> I live at 25 City Road, Delhi.
>
> My hobbies are cycling and football.
>
> Write and tell me all about yourself!

5 Ask the learners to rewrite the letter, putting the sentences in a better order (name, age, country, address, job, hobbies). Draw the letter layout below on the board and tell them to follow it.

6 When the learners have rewritten the letter, ask them to write a reply, telling the penpal all about themselves.

6 Countries

LANGUAGE	'Countries' (for example, **India**, **Greece**, **Japan**) and 'food' (for example, **curry**, **pizza**, **hamburgers**) vocabulary areas.
	_____ **is/ are from** _____ .
TECHNIQUES	Organizing texts: substitution. Creating texts: responding to a text.
MATERIALS	Substitution table, on a poster or on the board; menu, on a poster or on the board.
PREPARATION	Prepare the posters if you are using them.
TIME GUIDE	40 minutes.

Lead-in

1 Ask the learners if they have ever tried any of the following: curry, pizza, hamburgers, sushi, or chop suey. Ask them if they know which countries these kinds of food come from.

Organizing texts: substitution

2 Put up this substitution table.

Pizza	is	from	India.
Chop suey	are		Greece.
Moussaka			Japan.
Goulash			Italy.
Hamburgers			China.
Curry			Hungary.
Sushi			the USA.

3 Tell the learners to match the countries with the kinds of food, and then write seven correct sentences.

4 Check the answers with the whole class.

Creating texts: responding to a text

5 Put up this menu:

Welcome to the RENDEZVOUS INTERNATIONAL RESTAURANT.

From Italy, try our tasty pizzas. From Switzerland, we bring you fondue. From Greece, moussaka. Mmm. Delicious. A speciality from Turkey, kebabs. And from Thailand, spicy fish curry.

Explain any new vocabulary, for example, 'tasty', 'fondue', 'delicious', 'speciality', 'kebab', and 'spicy'.

6   Put the learners in pairs and ask them to discuss how they would lay out the menu to make it read and look better. Go round and help them while they are doing this.

7   Collect suggestions from the class and write up a new more attractive menu on the board. Ask the learners what they would choose to eat.

8   Put the learners in groups of three or four and ask them to design their own international menu.

9   When they have finished, get them to swap menus. Each group should then discuss what they would choose from their new menu. Write these speech bubbles on the board if you think they need support:

Mmm. I think I'll try _____.
What about you?

_____ sounds delicious.

Comment

If appropriate, change food items and their countries of origin to suit your learners' culture and general knowledge.

7 Nationalities

LANGUAGE	'Countries' (for example, **Canada**, **Japan**, **China**) and 'nationalities' (for example, **Canadian**, **Japanese**, **Chinese**) vocabulary areas.
TECHNIQUES	Organizing texts: completion. Creating texts: responding to a text.
MATERIALS	Lists and sentences, on a poster or on the board; letters, on a poster or on the board.
PREPARATION	Prepare the posters if you are using them.
TIME GUIDE	40 minutes.

Lead-in

1 Ask the learners about the nationalities of famous people they are likely to know; for example, pop stars, sportsmen and women, and political leaders.

Organizing texts: completion

2 Put up three lists, for example:

Country	Nationality	Languages
Canada	Venezuelan	French, German, and Italian
Japan	Swiss	Spanish
China	Canadian	Spanish
Mexico	Thai	French and English
Switzerland	Japanese	Chinese
Thailand	Russian	French and Arabic
Venezuela	Moroccan	Russian
Morocco	Chinese	Japanese
Russia	Mexican	Thai

Ask the learners to match country, nationality, and languages.

3 Put up some gap-fill sentences like the ones below. Tell the learners to copy them, filling in the gaps with words from the lists:

Carlos is _____ . He comes from Acapulco.

Su Rong Rong is _____ . She lives in Shanghai.

Begonis is a _____ . He lives in Caracas.

James is a _____ from Montreal. He speaks _____ and _____ .

Maria is _____ and comes from Lugano. She speaks _____ , _____ and _____ .

Jamila is _____ , from Marrakech. She speaks _____ and _____ .

**Creating texts:
responding to a text**

4 Put up these letters:

Hi!

I like music and films. I speak _____ and _____.
My name's Jean. I'm 23 years old. I'm Canadian. I live at 26
Avenue de Ternes, Montreal. How about you? Let me introduce
myself.

Hello!

I live in Shanghai, a big city in the east of _____. I'm Chinese.
My hobbies are reading and badminton. I like English! I speak
_____ and a little English. My name's Song Lin. How about
you?

Explain that the sentences in both letters are in the wrong order.
Go through the first one with the whole class, asking the learners to
reorder the sentences.

5 Get them to do the same with the other letter, working on their
own.

6 Ask for volunteers to read out their letters to the rest of the class.
Suggest corrections if necessary.

7 Ask the learners to choose one of the two letters and write a reply
to it. They can use language and sentence patterns from the letters
to help them.

Comment

If you feel that your learners are not familiar with the ones
presented here, substitute different countries and nationalities, and
adapt the letters.

8 Locating objects

LANGUAGE	'Everyday objects' (for example, **bag**, **vase**, **rose**) and 'classroom furniture' (for example **board**, **chair**, **table**) vocabulary areas.
	Place prepositions (for example, **on**, **next to**, **near**).
TECHNIQUES	Organizing texts: reordering. Creating texts: write and guess.
MATERIALS	Five sentences about objects in your classroom; description, on a poster or on the board.
PREPARATION	Prepare the sentences; prepare the poster if you are using one.
TIME GUIDE	40 minutes.

Lead-in

1 Write the first parts of the sentences about your classroom in a column on the left-hand side of the board and the second parts in jumbled order on the right-hand side, for example:

The blackboard is   on the chair.
My bag is   next to the door.
The table is   near the window.

Ask the learners to match the two parts to make sentences describing the classroom.

Organizing texts: reordering

2 Put up this description:

(1) On the table is a vase with one red rose in it. (2) The room is quite big. (3) There are two windows opposite the door. (4) Hanging from the ceiling, over the table are some balloons. (5) Next to the cake is a card saying 'I love you'. (6) Between the windows is a table. (7) In front of the vase is a big cake.

Ask the learners to read the text. Explain 'vase', 'rose', 'balloons', 'cake', and 'card' if necessary. Ask them what is going to happen in the room.

3 Get them to start drawing a picture of the room. Ask them how the text could be reordered to make it easier. Number the sentences and get the learners to decide what the best order would be to make the description clearer.

4 Go through their suggestions when they have finished (2, 3, 6, 1, 7, 5, 4 is the best, though 2, 3, 6, 4, 1, 7, 5 is possible). Ask the learners if any of the sentences can be joined with 'and'.

Creating texts:
write and guess

5 Tell the learners a riddle about an object in your classroom and ask them to guess what it is, for example:

It's next to the window, on the wall above the table. What is it?

another example:

It's on the table next to the door.

6 Get the learners to write five similar riddles about objects in the room, without mentioning the names of the objects.

7 When they have finished, put the learners in pairs and get them to read their riddles to each other. Their partners should guess what the objects are.

8 Ask for volunteers to read one of their riddles to the whole class, and let the class guess what the object is.

9 Feelings

LANGUAGE	'Feelings' vocabulary area (for example, **hot, thirsty, happy**). **And, or, but.**
TECHNIQUES	Organizing texts: joining. Creating texts: survey and report.
MATERIALS	Notes; a list of eight to ten adjectives in the 'feelings' vocabulary area.
PREPARATION	Prepare your list of adjectives.
TIME GUIDE	40 minutes.

Lead-in

1 Ask a few learners about their feelings, for example, 'Are you happy? Write their answers on the board in the following patterns:

[Name] is _____ and _____ .
[Name] isn't _____ or _____ .
[Name] is _____ but _____ .

For example:

Mark is hot and thirsty.
Anna isn't angry or bored.
Kate is hungry but happy.

2 Explain that 'and' is used to join two feelings that are similar, for example, two bad ones or two good ones. In a negative sentence 'or' is used instead of 'and'. 'But' is used to join two contrasting feelings.

Organizing texts: joining

3 Write these notes on the board:

Tim/ hungry/ thirsty
Maria/ not angry/ cold
Anna/ tired/ thirsty/ happy
Ben/ tired/ excited
Sara/ not tired/ bored

Ask the learners to expand them into sentences using 'and', 'or', or 'but'.

4 Ask the learners to make two sentences, one to describe themselves and the other to describe the person sitting next to them.

Creating texts: survey and report

5 Write the 'feelings' adjectives you have prepared on the board. Ask the learners questions about their feelings using the adjectives, for example:

> Who is happy today?
> How many of you are hot?
> How many of you are cold?

Write the totals on the board, for example:

Happy	32
Hot	37
Cold	1
Bored	0
Angry	0

6 Tell the learners to write the results as a survey, for example:

In Class Three today, thirty-two people are happy. Thirty-seven people are hot, but one person is cold! No-one is bored or angry.

10 Families

LANGUAGE

'Families' vocabulary area (for example, **mother, father, brother**).

On the right; in the middle; on the left.
He/ she's a _____ .

TECHNIQUES

Organizing texts: reordering.
Creating texts: writing from a picture.

MATERIALS

Photographs of learners' families; board drawing of your family; description, on a poster or on the board; sentence frames.

PREPARATION

At the end of the previous lesson, ask the learners to bring a photograph of their family to the next lesson. Make a sketch for a board drawing of your family. Spend a little time preparing what you're going to say about each member of your family. Prepare the poster if you are using one.

TIME GUIDE

40 minutes

Lead-in

1 Draw a picture of your family on the board. As you draw, talk about each member, for example:

This is a picture of my family. This is me [*draw self*] —in the middle, look, and here is my husband standing next to me. [*draw husband*] On the right are my husband's parents. [*draw parents*] This is his mother, and this is his father. They're both teachers … etc.

Constructing texts: reordering

2 Put up this text:

(1) This is our wedding photo.

(2) On the left are my mother and father—both 65 and retired now.

(3) That's us—in the middle of the picture.

(4) Next to my parents are my brothers—Michael and his wife Jill, and Hugh and his wife Anne.

(5) Michael is an engineer, and Hugh and Anne are both doctors.

(6) Next to my father-in-law is my wife's sister, Felicity, and her baby son.

(7) Next to Felicity, on the far right of the picture, are my wife's cousins, Lynn and John.

(8) At the end of the row, next to Hugh, is a surprise guest—my sister Susan.

(9) On the right is my wife's family—her mother and father are standing next to her.

(10) Susan lives in America, but she came over for the wedding.

Ask the learners to read the text and to try to draw the photo. Ask them if it would be easier if the sentences were in a different order. Discuss how the text could be better arranged so that the reader can visualize it better.

3 Get the learners to write down the order they think would be the clearest.

4 Collect suggestions from the class. Working out from the middle towards the left and then towards the right (1, 3, 2, 4, 5, 8, 10, 9, 6, 7), or towards the right and then towards the left (1, 3, 9, 6, 7, 2, 4, 5, 8, 10) are probably the best.

Creating texts: writing from a picture

5 Write these sentence frames on the board. Tell the learners to use them to write sentences about their photos.

My ＿＿＿ is on the right.

My ＿＿＿ is on the left.

My ＿＿＿ is in the middle of the photograph.

Behind my ＿＿＿ is my ＿＿＿.

In front of my ＿＿＿ is my ＿＿＿.

His/ her name is ＿＿＿.

He/ she's ＿＿＿.

He/ she's a ＿＿＿.

6 Get the learners to work in pairs, describing their photographs to each other.

11 Colours

LANGUAGE	'Colours' vocabulary area (for example, **blue**, **red**, **green**). **What colour is the _____?** **It's _____ .**
TECHNIQUES	Organizing texts: reordering. Creating texts: responding to a text.
MATERIALS	Eight flashcards of the illustrations below; poem with lines in jumbled order, on a poster or on the board; poem with lines in the correct order, on a poster or on the board.
PREPARATION	Make the flashcards. Make the posters if you are using them.
TIME GUIDE	50 minutes.

Lead-in

1 Hold up the flashcards one by one, and ask the learners what colour each thing is.

2 Fix the flashcards to the board in a row. Write the name of each colour above the pictures and the name of each thing below it. For example:

blue red
sea apple

Put the learners in pairs and ask them to think of as many other things as they can which are the same colours as the things on the flashcards. Supply vocabulary if they need it.

3 Write the learners' suggestions below the flashcards.

Organizing texts: reordering

4 Teach these words with quick sketches on the board: 'rose', 'poppy', 'swan', 'pear', 'grass', 'cloud', 'fountain', 'barley', 'clouds', and 'twilight'. Some of the things may be unfamiliar to your learners. Just explain that they are English flowers/ birds/ fruit/ crops. If you can, try to find a local flower, fruit etc. that is similar.

5 Put up this poem. Explain that the lines in the left-hand column are already in the correct order, but those in the right-hand column are in jumbled order. Also tell the learners that the poem rhymes.

What is pink?

What is pink? A rose is pink
By the fountain's brink.

What is red? A poppy's red   Sailing in the light.
What is blue? The sky is blue   In its barley bed.
What is white? A swan is white   In the summer twilight.
What is yellow? Pears are yellow   Just an orange!
What is green? The grass is green   Where the clouds float through.
What is violet? Clouds are violet   Rich and ripe and mellow.
What is orange? Why, an orange   With small flowers between.

Ask the learners to put the lines in the correct order.

Creating text: responding to a text

6 Put up the poem with the lines in the correct order. (It is by the Victorian poet, Christina Rossetti).

What is pink?

What is pink? A rose is pink   What is yellow? Pears are yellow
By the fountain's brink.   Rich and ripe and mellow.
What is red? A poppy's red   What is green? The grass is green
In its barley bed.   With small flowers between.
What is blue? The sky is blue   What is violet? Clouds are violet
Where the clouds float through.   In the summer twilight.
What is white? A swan is white   What is orange? Why, an orange
Sailing in the light.   Just an orange!

7 Ask the learners to write their own poem on the same pattern, using the words and ideas they collected in the Lead-in. Show them how the pairs of lines should be structured:

What is _____? _____ is/ are _____

_____ .

Tell them that their poems don't have to rhyme!

8 Ask for volunteers to read out their poems to the rest of the class.

12 Shapes

LANGUAGE	'Shapes' (for example, **square**, **round**, **long**) and 'colours' (for example, **brown**, **red**, **black**) vocabulary areas.
	And, with.
TECHNIQUES	Organizing texts: substitution. Creating texts: write and guess.
MATERIALS	Exercises, on a poster or on the board.
PREPARATION	Make the poster if you are using one.
TIME GUIDE	40 minutes.

Lead-in

1   Describe two or three of things in the room, for example:

> It's square and brown with four legs.
> It's small and round and red, with money inside.

Get the learners to guess what you are describing (table, purse).

Organizing texts: substitution

2   Write a substitution table on the board like the one below. Ask the learners to write five sentences from the table.

A	pencil				red.
An	books	is	long	and	thick.
	apple	are	square		black.
	bananas		round		yellow.
	blackboard				thin.

3   Go round the class and check the learners' work.

**Creating texts:
write and guess**

4 Put up these exercises:

A Join these short sentences into one longer sentence using 'and':

It's yellow. It's long. It's curved.

It's black. It's square. It's big.

It's round. It's flat. It's silver.

B Join these short sentences into one longer sentence using 'with':

It's long and thin and round. It has a pointed end.

It's long and very thin and silver. It has a point at one end and a very small hole at the other.

It's round and gold. It has a hole in the middle.

Ask the learners to do them.

5 Check the sentences with the whole class. Ask the learners if they can guess what the objects are (**A** banana, board, coin; **B** pencil, needle, ring).

6 Put the learners into pairs and ask them to make up some riddles of their own like the ones in the exercise.

7 When each pair has made up at least two riddles, join the pairs into groups of four and ask them to read out their riddles for the other pair to guess.

13 Parts of the body

LANGUAGE	'Parts of the body' vocabulary area (for example, **foot**, **head**, **knee**).
TECHNIQUES	Organizing texts: joining. Creating texts: write and draw.
MATERIALS	Drawing and description of a robot, on a poster or on the board; two pieces of paper for each of the learners.
PREPARATION	Make the poster if you are using one.
TIME GUIDE	40 minutes.

Lead-in

1 Call out parts of the body, for example, 'Foot!', 'Head!', 'Knee!' Tell the learners to point to that part of their body, as quickly as they can. Increase your speed as you go on.

Organizing texts: matching and joining

2 Put up these pictures and descriptions and ask the learners to match them.

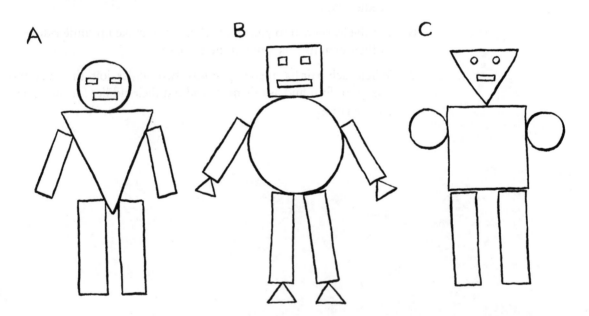

A   B   C

1 This robot has a square head and a round body. Its arms and legs are rectangular. It has triangular hands and feet.

2 This robot has a triangular head. Its body is square and it has round arms and rectangular legs.

3 This robot has a round head and a triangular body. It has rectangular arms and legs.

3 Check the answers with the class. (1–B, 2–C, 3–A).

4 Put up this robot and the description of it.

Its body is rectangular	and	round eyes and a triangular mouth.
Its hands and feet are triangular	with	it has ten fingers on each hand.
The robot has a square head		it has four arms and three legs.

Ask the learners to match the sentence halves in the description, joining them with 'and' or 'with'.

5 Ask them what they think is the best order for the sentences to make a description of the picture. This is probably:

The robot has a square head with round eyes and a triangular mouth. Its body is rectangular and it has four arms and three legs. Its hands and feet are triangular and it has ten fingers on each hand (i.e. describing from the top downwards).

Creating texts: write and draw

6 Give each learner two sheets of paper. Tell them to draw their own robot on one sheet, and to write a description of it on the other.

7 When they have finished, put them in pairs. Tell them to give the description, but not the drawing, to their partner. Their partner should read the description and try to draw the robot. They can then compare their drawings.

14 Describing people

LANGUAGE 'Describing people' (for example, **tall**, **slim**), 'parts of the body' (for example, **hair**, **face**, **nose**), and 'colours' (for example, **blonde**, **blue**, **black**) vocabulary areas.

TECHNIQUES Organizing texts: writing from notes.
Creating texts: visualization.

MATERIALS Police poster, on a poster or on the board.

PREPARATION Make the poster if you are using one.

TIME GUIDE 40 minutes.

Lead-in

1 Ask the learners to close their eyes and to think of a famous person. Tell them to think of what the person looks like. Then they should open their eyes and describe him or her to the person sitting next to them, who should try to guess who it is.

Organizing texts: writing from notes

2 Put up this police poster and write the notes beside it on the board:

tall
slim
long curly blonde hair
round face
blue eyes
long nose
black dress

3 Write this outline description on the board. Ask the learners to expand the notes beside the poster into a description based on the outline:

Police are looking for a woman last seen in a red car near West Street.
—height
—shape
—hair
—face
—eyes
—nose
—clothes.
Anyone who sees the woman should contact the police immediately.

4 Ask some learners to read out their descriptions. Discuss different ways of describing the woman, for example:

The woman is tall and slim with long curly blonde hair, a round face, blue eyes and a long nose. She is wearing a black dress.

or:

The woman is tall and slim. She has long, curly blonde hair and a round face, with blue eyes and a long nose. She is wearing a black dress.

Creating texts: visualization

5 Ask the learners to visualize their ideal man or woman. Ask them what he or she would look like. (With younger children you can ask them to imagine fairy-tale characters, for example, a prince or a princess.) Elicit some vocabulary and write it on the board.

6 Ask learners to write a short description of the person.

7 Put the learners in pairs, or groups of three, to compare their descriptions.

8 Ask the groups to report back to the class, for example: 'Sara's ideal man is tall and dark, but mine is blonde with a beard.'

15 Clothes

LANGUAGE	'Clothes' (for example, **sweater, jacket, jeans**), 'colours' (for example, **red, green, blue**), and 'describing people' (for example, **tall, small, fat**) vocabulary areas.
TECHNIQUES	Organizing texts: reordering and joining. Creating texts: write and do.
MATERIALS	Sentences, on a poster or on the board; a bag of clothes for dressing up as robbers; another bag, marked 'money'.
PREPARATION	Make the poster if you are using one. Prepare the clothes.
TIME GUIDE	40 minutes.

Lead-in

1 Divide the class into two teams. Choose and say an item of clothing that one of the learners is wearing, for example, 'a red shirt'. The first team to say the name of the person wearing that item gets a point. Continue for about ten items of clothing. You can let a volunteer from the class call out items of clothing.

Organizing texts: reordering and joining

2 Put up these sentences. Ask the learners what they think the best order for the sentences would be. Tell them to write out the sentences in the best order, and to combine some of them with 'and'.

1 The other had a red sweater.

2 The tall man had a green jacket and blue jeans.

3 He had black trousers.

4 I saw two young men running down the street at about six o'clock.

5 Both men were wearing trainers.

6 The other was smaller and fattish.

7 One was tall.

8 He was quite slim.

9 Both men had short brown hair.

3 Put them in pairs and get them to read each others' descriptions. Collect suggestions from the class and agree on the best order for the sentences. (4, 8, 7, 6, 9, 2, 1, 3, 5 is probably the best order. 1 and 3 can be combined with 'and', and so can 7 and 8.)

Creating texts: write and do

4 Tell the learners that you need some actors, and ask for four or five volunteers. Ask them to come outside the door with you. Tell them that they are bank robbers, and that they are going to act out a robbery. Give them the bag of clothes you have brought in, and ask them to disguise themselves. They can also swap some of their own clothes if they like. Then tell them that the classroom is a bank, and that you are a cashier. You will be sitting at your desk. After one minute they should run in and demand money. You will give it to them, and they should take it and run out again.

5 Go back into the class and tell them, 'This is a bank and I am the cashier.' Ask a few learners to come up and stand in a queue at the desk. Pretend to be dealing with the first 'customer' when the 'robbers' run in.

6 When the 'robbers' have taken the money and gone out again, ask the class to discuss in pairs what they saw. Ask them if they can remember what the robbers were wearing, and then tell them to write a description of what they saw for the police.

7 When the robbers have changed into their normal clothes and come back into the room, tell them to try and remember what they were all wearing, and write a description too.

8 Get the learners to work in pairs or small groups and discuss what they have written. Ask them if all their descriptions of the robbers are the same.

9 Get feedback about the descriptions from the whole class.

16 Rooms

LANGUAGE	'Rooms' vocabulary area (for example, **living-room**, **bedroom**, **kitchen**).
	On the right; on the left.
	Place prepositions.
TECHNIQUES	Organizing texts: matching. Creating texts: visualization.
MATERIALS	Pictures of houses, on a poster or on the board; plan of a flat, on a poster or on the board.
PREPARATION	Make the posters if you are using them.
TIME GUIDE	40 minutes.

....

Lead-in **1** Put up these pictures:

Make sure the learners know the words for the different kinds of house. Ask them which they would like to live in most, and why.

....

Organizing texts: matching **2** Put up the plan of a flat, and the half sentences:

The living-room	is	next to the bedroom.
The kitchen		next to the kitchen.
The bathroom		at the end of the hall.
The kitchen		on the left.
The living-room		between the living-room and the bathroom.
The bedroom		between the bedroom and the kitchen.
The bathroom		on the right of the hall.

Get the learners to match sentence halves to make true sentences about the plan. They should mention all the rooms in the flat.

3 Tell them to arrange their sentences to make a description of the flat.

4 Ask some of the learners to read out their descriptions to the rest of the class.

Creating texts: visualization

5 Ask the learners to choose a house from the first poster. Get them to close their eyes and visualize what it would be like inside. Ask them questions such as:

How many rooms are there?
What are the names of the rooms?

6 Tell them to open their eyes and write a description of their imaginary house.

7 Put the learners in pairs. They should read their descriptions to their partners, who should try and guess what kind of home they have described.

17 Furniture

LANGUAGE	'Furniture' (for example, **sofa, table, bed**) and 'rooms' (for example, **living-room, kitchen, bedroom**) vocabulary areas.
	Place prepositions.
TECHNIQUES	Organizing texts: completion.
	Creating texts: write and draw.
MATERIALS	Drawing and description of room, on a poster or on the board.
PREPARATION	Make the poster if you are using one.
TIME GUIDE	40 minutes.

Lead-in

1   Write this substitution table on the board:

There	is	a	sofa	in the	living-room.
	isn't	some	table		kitchen.
	are	any	bed		bedroom.
	aren't	cooker		hall.	
			cupboards		
			chairs		
			armchairs		

Ask the learners to make sentences orally that are true for the flat or house where they live.

Organizing texts: completion

2   Put up this drawing and extract from a letter:

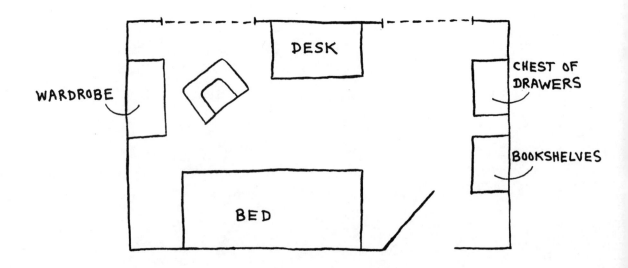

. . . and they've given me a room on the second floor. I'm very pleased with it. It's quite a big room and very light, because there are two windows overlooking the garden. My desk is _____ the windows and my bed is against the wall _____ the desk. There's an armchair _____ the desk and _____ the chair there's a wardrobe. _____ them, there's a chest of drawers with bookshelves _____ to it. Everything I need really!

3 Write these prepositions on the board:

near   opposite (x2)   next   between   behind

Tell the learners to fill in the blanks with the correct prepositions.

4 Check the answers with the whole class.

5 Discuss how the text is organized. Ask the learners:

What did the letter writer describe first?
Why do you think she chose that?

Ask them how the writer made it easy to visualize the room. (The writer described the most important things in the room first—the windows and the desk between them—the things that would catch your eye when you went in. She then went on to describe where other things were in relation to the windows and the desk.)

Creating texts: write and draw

6 Ask the learners to imagine that they have moved into a new room, or redecorated a room in their house. (For younger learners you can ask them to imagine they have found a wizard's room, or a princess's room in a castle.) Ask them to draw a picture of the room, and to write a letter to a friend about it. They can use the vocabulary and sentence patterns from the substitution table and the description to help them.

7 Ask them to exchange letters with a partner, and to try to draw their partner's room. They can then compare their drawings.

18 In town

LANGUAGE
'Town' vocabulary area (for example, **post office, cafe, bank**).

On the right; on the left.

Place prepositions (for example, **next to, beside, opposite**).

TECHNIQUES
Organizing texts: reordering.
Creating texts: write and draw.

MATERIALS
Drawing of the alien town and the letter, on a poster or on the board.

PREPARATION
Make the poster if you are using one.

TIME GUIDE
40 minutes.

Lead-in

1   Tell the learners to close their eyes and imagine they are walking down the main street of their town. Ask them questions, for example:

> What can you see?
> What is on the right?
> What is on the left?

Give them a short time to imagine, then ask them to stop 'walking' and open their eyes. Ask them to tell the person sitting next to them where they are in the street.

Organizing texts: reordering

2   Put up this picture, and extract from a 'letter from Planet Zeta':

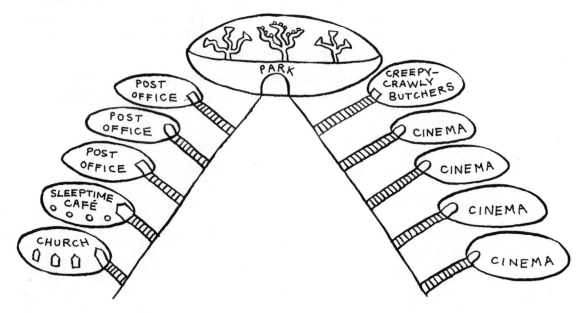

1 Here's a picture of the main street in my town.

2 Next to the post offices is a cafe where we go to drink Snoozola and have a good sleep (Snoozola gives you nice dreams!).

3 There aren't any banks in Zeta, because no one needs money .

4 Next to it, on the right, is a butcher's where we get our beetles and worms.

5 At the far end is the park, where we all go to fly around and have fun.

6 On the other side of the street are three post offices—we Zetans write a lot of letters!

7 Beside the cafe is the church, where we all go to dance on Thursdays.

8 There aren't any bookshops because we don't have books, but there are four cinemas opposite the post offices.

Tell the learners to look at the picture and put the sentences in the best order to make a clear description. Ask them whether they can link any of them with 'and'.

3 When they have finished, tell them to compare their texts with a partner.

4 Go through the description with the whole class (the best order is probably 1, 5, 4, 6, 2, 7, 3, 8).

Creating texts: write and draw

5 Ask the learners to write a reply to the alien's letter. They can either describe their real main street, or imagine they live on another planet and describe an imaginary street. In either case, tell them to draw a plan of the street before they start, to help them organize their description.

6 Put the learners in pairs. Tell them to exchange descriptions with their partners, and to try and draw each other's descriptions. They can then compare their drawings.

19 Directions

LANGUAGE   'Town' vocabulary area (for example, **station, cinema, park**).

Go straight on.
Turn right.
Turn left.
Take the second on the right.
Take the third on the left.

TECHNIQUES   Organizing texts: completion.
Creating texts: write and draw.

MATERIALS   Map of the area around your house, and letter, on a poster or on the board; sheet of paper for each learner.

PREPARATION   Make the poster if you are using one.

TIME GUIDE   40 minutes.

....

Lead-in   **1**   Put the learners in pairs. Ask them to describe their route to school or work to each other.

....

Organizing texts: completion   **2**   Put up a sketch map of the area around your house, with a short letter to a friend giving directions for finding it. Leave blanks for the direction words. Here is an example.

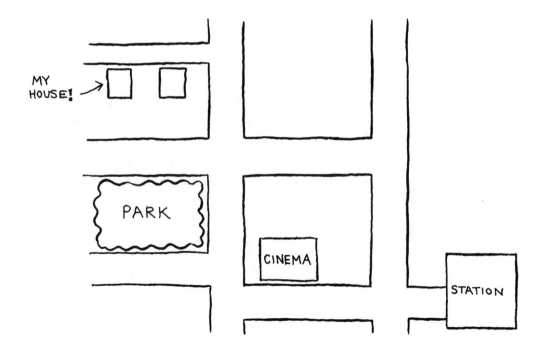

Dear Helen,

Here's the map that you asked for. When you leave the station, go _____ on, past the cinema. At the end of the road _____ right. Go straight on, _____ the park and take the _____ turning on the _____. My house is the _____ house on the _____.

See you soon!
Anna

Tell the learners to read the letter, and to use the map to help them fill in the blanks.

3 Tell them to check their answers with the person sitting next to them.

4 Check the answers with the whole class.

....

Creating texts: write and draw

5 Ask the learners to imagine that a friend is coming to see them, but doesn't know how to get to their flat or house. Tell them to draw a map of the area round their flat or house, but tell them not to mark the flat or house on it. They should then write a letter giving directions on how to find where they live. They can use language from the letter to Helen to help them.

6 Put the learners in pairs and get them to exchange letters and maps. They should read their partner's letter and use it to help them mark the flat or house on the map.

7 Get feedback from the class. Was it easy to mark the flats or houses from the descriptions in the letters?

20 In the market

LANGUAGE	'Food' vocabulary area (for example, **apples**, **cheese**, **bread**). **Some, any.**
TECHNIQUES	Organizing texts: substitution. Creating texts: write and guess.
MATERIALS	Substitution table, on the board; poem and framework, on two posters or on the board.
PREPARATION	Make the posters if you are using them.
TIME GUIDE	40 minutes.

Lead-in

1 Ask the learners to close their eyes and visualize a market. Tell them to imagine they are walking round it. Ask them what they can see for sale.

2 Ask for volunteers to tell the rest of the class what they 'saw' in the market.

Constructing texts: substitution

3 Write this substitution table on the board. (If necessary, adapt the table to show food items that learners are likely to know.)

There	is	a	apples	in the	market.
	isn't	some	cheese		
	are	any	bread		
	aren't		melon		
			fish		
			oil		
			milk		

Tell the learners to use the table to write sentences that are true about the market they visualized.

4 Ask the learners if there were any other kinds of food in their market. Add them to the substitution table.

5 Tell the learners to write a description of their market using the sentences they have made, and new sentences with the other kinds of food they have suggested.

**Creating texts:
write and guess**

6 Put up this poem:

In the market

I bought some eggs,
I bought some cheese,
I bought a little ham,
But I didn't buy any peas.
I went back home and opened my book—
What kind of meal am I going to cook?

Ask the learners to read the poem, then ask them what they think you are going to make with the ingredients. (a ham and cheese omelette)

7 Ask the learners to think of a simple recipe they know, and to write down a list of the ingredients.

8 Put up this framework:

In the market

I bought _____
I bought _____
I bought _____
(etc., as often as necessary)
But I didn't buy _____.
I went back home and opened my book—
What kind of meal am I going to cook?

Tell the learners to make their own poems, using the framework and the ingredients they have written down.

9 When they have finished, put them in groups of three or four and get them to read their poems to each other. They should try to guess what dish each of them is going to cook.

21 Shopping

LANGUAGE	'Containers' and 'food and drink' vocabulary areas (for example, **a pot of yoghurt, a loaf of bread, a can of beer**).
TECHNIQUES	Organizing texts: substitution. Creating texts: write and guess.
MATERIALS	Substitution table, on a poster or on the board; instructions on slips of paper.
PREPARATION	Make the poster, if you are using one; prepare the instructions on slips of paper.
TIME GUIDE	40 minutes.

Lead-in

1 Divide the class into two teams. Say the name of a container, for example, 'bottle'. The first team to name something that comes in that container (for example, 'milk' in a bottle) gets a point.

2 Continue for eight to ten containers. The team with the most points at the end is the winner.

Organizing texts: substitution

3 Put up this substitution table:

A	bar		toothpaste
Two	pots		bread
Six	tube		yoghurt
Three	cans	of	potatoes
	loaves		beer
	packet		jam
	jar		chocolate
	bag		tea

4 Tell the learners to match the containers with the items of food and drink, and write a shopping list.

Creating texts:
write and guess

5 Ask the learners to think of the people in their family. What is each person's favourite food or drink? Ask them to write a shopping list for the family containing each person's favourite, for example:

6 cans of beer   (my father)
5 bags of sweets   (my little sister)
10 bars of chocolate (me!)

6 Get them to compare their lists with their neighbour.

7 Divide the learners into groups of four. Give each learner in each group one of these four instructions on a slip of paper:

Write a shopping list for an old person living on their own.
Write a shopping list for a family of six.
Write a shopping list for a party.
Write a shopping list for a special meal.

The learners should not show their slips of paper to the others in the group.

8 Tell the learners to write a shopping list for the person or situation described on their slip.

9 When they have finished, get them to read out their lists to the others in the group. The others must guess who the list is for.

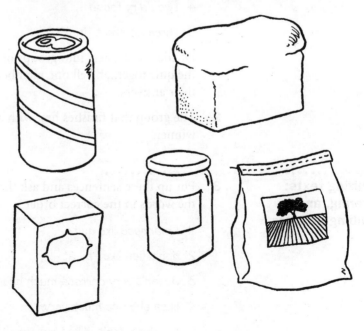

22 Food and drink

LANGUAGE   'Food and drink' vocabulary area (for example, **mangoes, fish, carrots**).

I like/ don't like _____ .
He/ she likes/ doesn't like _____ .

Very much; quite; not very much; not at all.

TECHNIQUES   Organizing texts: reordering, and describing pictures.
Creating texts: responding to a text.

MATERIALS   Sentences, on a poster or on the board; picture clues, on a poster or on the board.

PREPARATION   Prepare the posters, if you are using them.

TIME GUIDE   40 minutes.

Lead-in

1   Write up this quiz on the board:

Name:
1 four kinds of fruit

2 three kinds of vegetable

3 three kinds of meat

4 two dairy foods

5 three different drinks

Divide the learners into groups of three or four and tell them to do the quiz together. Tell one member of each group to write down their answers.

2   The group that finishes first with all the answers correct is the winner.

Organizing texts: reordering, and describing pictures

3   Put up these sentences and ask the learners to rewrite them, putting the words in the correct order:

1 I mangoes like quite

2 don't fish like I all at

3 doesn't very carrots much he like

4 likes she rice much very

5 like duck don't I like I but very chicken much at all

4 Write the sentences in the correct order on the board, and tell the learners to check their work.

5 Put up these picture clues:

6 Tell the learners to use them to write sentences with the same patterns as those they have just completed.

Creating texts: responding to a text

7 Ask the learners to write a letter to a penpal in another country, telling him or her about the kinds of food they eat. They should say which kinds of food they like and don't like, using the sentence patterns they have practised.

23 Leisure activities

LANGUAGE   'Leisure activities' vocabulary area (for example, **swimming, sewing, football**).

TECHNIQUES   Organizing texts: substitution.
Creating texts: survey and report.

MATERIALS   Substitution table, on the board; charts.

PREPARATION   Choose some leisure activities that are familiar to your learners. Make the charts.

TIME GUIDE   50 minutes.

....
Lead-in

Ask the learners to tell you the names of activities they enjoy doing in their free time. Translate for them if they can't think of the word in English. Write the activities in a list on the right-hand side of the board.

....
Organizing texts: substitution

1 Change the list into a substitution table like this:

I My partner	like/ likes don't mind/ doesn't mind hate/ hates	(list of activities)

2 Divide the learners into pairs. Tell them to use the table to write sentences that are true (and correct!) for themselves and their partners.

3 Ask some learners to report back to the rest of the class. They should tell you one thing about their partner and one about themselves.

....
Creating texts: survey and report

4 Change the substitution table back into a list by rubbing out the two left-hand columns.

5 Tell the learners to copy the list and make a chart like this (demonstrate on the board):

	likes	doesn't mind	hates
(list of activities)			

6 Divide the class into groups of six to eight learners, and write the following prompts on the board:

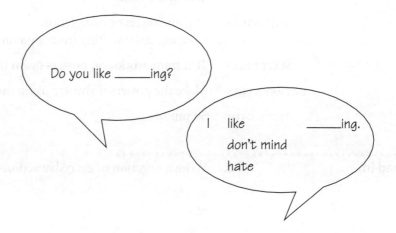

Do you like _____ing?

I like _____ing.
don't mind
hate

7 Tell the learners to find out what the other members of their group feel about each leisure activity listed on their charts. They should note the number of people who like, don't mind, or hate each activity, for example:

	likes	doesn't mind	hates
swimming	4	2	2
sewing	1	2	5
dancing	6	1	1

8 Ask each group to report back to the rest of the class which was the most popular and which was the least popular activity in their group.

9 Write this framework on the board:

In a survey of leisure activities in our group we found that _____ is the favourite activity. The next most popular activity is _____. Less popular activities are _____, _____, and _____. The least popular activities are _____ and _____.

Tell the learners to write reports of their surveys using their charts and the framework.

24 Daily routines

LANGUAGE	'Everyday activities' vocabulary area (for example, **get up**, **wash**, **have breakfast**).
	Telling the time.
TECHNIQUES	Organizing texts: completion.
	Creating texts: writing from a picture.
MATERIALS	Text frameworks, on posters or on the board; flashcards of animals.
PREPARATION	Make the posters if you are using them; make the flashcards.
TIME GUIDE	50 minutes.

Lead-in

1 Write a selection of everyday actions on the board, for example:

watch TV
read
cook
do housework
do homework

Tell the learners you are going to do a quick survey to find out what they do in the evenings.

2 Read out each action. Ask the learners to put up their hands if they do it regularly in the evenings. Count the hands and write the total by each action. What do most learners do?

Organizing texts: completion

3 Put up this text framework:

Every day I _____ _____ at _____ _____ . First I _____ and then I _____ . Then I _____ . After that I _____ to school. I _____ _____ at _____ _____ and I go home at _____ _____ . In the evening I _____ and then I _____ . I _____ to bed at _____ _____ .

Tell the learners to copy and complete it for a typical day in their lives. If you have a class that needs more support, you can give suggestions for filling in some of the gaps, for example:

brush my teeth
go
have supper
get up
have lunch
wash
have breakfast

4 Put up this text framework and ask the learners to describe what they do after school:

I get home from school at _____.
First I _____ and then I _____.
Next I _____ and _____.
After that I sometimes _____ or _____.
I go to bed at _____.

Creating texts: writing from a picture

5 Show the learners flashcards of four or five different kinds of animal, for example:

Choose animals that are familiar to your learners.

6 Ask the learners to choose one and to write a description of a typical day from that animal's point of view. They can use the framework for the description of their own day to help them.

7 When they have finished, put the learners in pairs to read their descriptions to each other and to guess which animal's day is being described.

25 Jobs

LANGUAGE	'Jobs' vocabulary area (for example, **farmer**, **doctor**, **waiter**).
TECHNIQUES	Organizing texts: substitution.
	Creating texts: write and guess.
MATERIALS	Model text on a poster.
PREPARATION	Make the poster.
TIME GUIDE	50 minutes.

....

Lead-in

1 Put the learners in groups of three or four. Tell the groups that they must think of as many jobs as they can in three minutes. One learner in each group should write down the jobs.

2 Write the jobs the learners have thought of on the board. The group which has thought of the most jobs is the winner.

....

Organizing texts: substitution

3 Put up this model description:

My	father	is a	_____.
	mother		
	brother		
	sister		

He	wears	a uniform.
She		a suit.
		overalls.
		casual clothes.
		an apron.
		a white coat.

He	gets up	very early.
She	doesn't get up	

He	comes home at about _____ o'clock.
She	

He	likes	his	boss.
She	doesn't like	her	

He	earns	a lot of money.
She	doesn't earn	

Ask the learners to write about a member of their family, or a friend, using the model.

....

**Creating texts:
write and guess**

4 Ask the learners to choose one of the jobs on the board, and to write a description of a day in the life of a person who does that job. Tell them not to mention the name of the job in their descriptions. Tell them that they can use sentence patterns from the model text.

5 When they have finished writing, put the learners in groups of three or four, and tell them to swap their descriptions.

6 They should read the descriptions they have been given, and guess which job is being described.

....

Comment

You can choose jobs that your learners are familiar with, and that are culturally appropriate.

26 Housework

LANGUAGE	'Housework' vocabulary area (for example, **wash the dishes**, **make the beds**, **do the shopping**.
	To hate (doing something).
TECHNIQUES	Organizing texts: describing a picture, and completion. Creating texts: write and draw.
MATERIALS	Poster of a 'kitchen robot'.
PREPARATION	Make the poster.
TIME GUIDE	50 minutes.

Lead-in

1 Write a selection of household tasks on the board, for example:

wash the dishes
make the beds
do the shopping

Tell the learners you are going to do a quick survey to find out which household task they hate the most.

2 Read out each task. Ask the learners 'Who hates _____ most?' Tell them to put up their hands. Write the total by each task. What do the largest number of learners hate doing?

Organizing texts: describing a picture, and completion

3 Put up this picture and text:

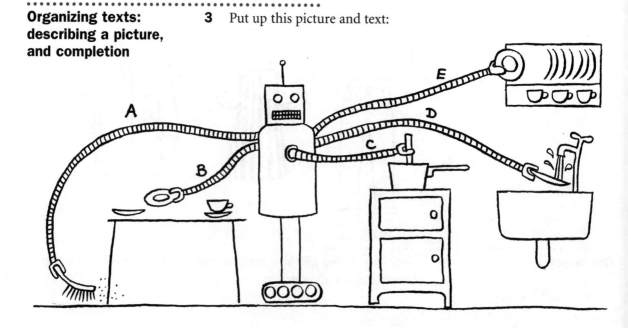

Introducing Robocook, the amazing kitchen robot. Do you hate cooking? Do you loathe washing up? Do you sometimes long for help? Don't despair! Help is here! Robo's arms help with all those boring kitchen tasks. Arm A _____ , while Arm B _____ , and Arm C _____ . After the meal Arm D _____ and Arm E _____ . Robocook is always ready to help! He is never tired! he never grumbles! Buy one today!

Tell the learners to look at the picture and write out the text, filling in the gaps. If necessary, help them by writing the tasks Robocook is doing on the board:

laying the table
washing the dishes
sweeping the floor
putting the dishes away
cooking the dinner

4 Get the learners to check their answers in pairs.

5 Go through the answers with the whole class.

**Creating texts:
write and draw**

6 Tell the learners to invent a machine to help them with a household task they hate doing. Ask them to draw their machine and to write a short paragraph describing it.

7 Put the learners in pairs and tell them to show their pictures and read their descriptions to each other.

27 Abilities

LANGUAGE	'Abilities' (for example, **drive**, **sing**, **cook**) and 'jobs' (for example, **bus driver**, **secretary**, **doctor**) vocabulary areas.
	Can.
TECHNIQUES	Organizing texts: reordering. Creating texts: write and do.
MATERIALS	Job adverts poster; letter of application poster; pieces of paper with the names of jobs for all the learners.
PREPARATION	Make the posters.
TIME GUIDE	60 minutes.

Lead-in

1 Write a list of jobs on the board, for example:

bus driver   doctor   businessman/ woman   teacher
secretary   farmer   hairdresser

2 Divide the class into two teams and give a clue to one of the jobs using 'can', for example: 'She can cure people' (doctor); 'She can type' (secretary). The first team to give the correct answer gets a point.

3 The team with the most points at the end is the winner.

Organizing texts: reordering

4 Put up this poster of job adverts:

Then put up this letter:

> Dear Sir,
>
> I can drive, sing, cook delicious meals, wash clothes and dishes, sew, knit, and tell good stories. I hope you will consider my application. I can work twenty-four hours a day, seven days a week. I would like to apply for the job of _____. I have five pairs of arms for hugging, five pairs of eyes for watching, five pairs of ears for listening, and five mouths for singing songs and telling stories.
>
> Yours faithfully,

5 Explain any unfamiliar vocabulary, and then ask the learners which job the writer is applying for (mother).

6 Ask them to write out the letter, putting the sentences in a better order.

7 Check the order of the sentences with the whole class (4, 1, 5, 3, 2, or possibly 4, 3, 1, 5, 2).

Creating texts: write and do

8 Give each learner a piece of paper with the name of one of the other jobs on it.

9 Tell them to write a letter of application for the job on their piece of paper. They should use the letter they have copied as a model. Go round and help them while they are writing, supplying any vocabulary they need.

10 Collect up the letters in sets, i.e. all the zoo keeper applications, all the clown applications, and so on.

11 Divide the class into groups. These groups are 'assessment boards' for each of the jobs. Give each board their set of applications. Tell the groups to read all their applications and to decide who gets the job.

28 Rules: 'must' and 'mustn't'

LANGUAGE	**Must, mustn't.**
TECHNIQUES	Constructing texts: matching. Creating texts: write and guess.
MATERIALS	Lists of places.
PREPARATION	Prepare enough lists of places for the sub-groups.
TIME GUIDE	50 minutes.

Lead-in

1 Ask the learners 'What are the rules at home? What do your parents tell you you *must* do? What do they tell you you *mustn't* do?' (If your learners are adults, ask them to remember their childhood.)

2 Put them in groups of three or four to talk about this. Then ask the groups to report back to the rest of the class.

Constructing texts: matching

3 Write these half sentences on the board:

You must	shout
You mustn't	run in the corridors
	eat in class
	be late
	be polite
	do your homework
	climb out of the windows
	write on the textbooks

4 Ask for volunteers to make complete sentences. Ask them what the sentences might be called ('School rules').

5 Get the learners to write out eight complete sentences. They should give their sentences the title 'School rules'.

6 Check the answers with the whole class.

Creating texts: write and guess

7 Divide the class into groups of four or five. Then divide each group into two pairs, or a pair and a group of three (A and B).

8 Give As in each group this list of places: aeroplane, hospital, shop, zoo. Give Bs in each group this list of places: prison, bank, park, boat.

9 Ask the learners to write a set of rules for each place. Give them an example, in a library the rules might look like this:

LIBRARY

You must talk quietly.

You mustn't eat or drink.

You mustn't run.

You must return books
on time.

Go round and help, supplying any necessary vocabulary.

10 Ask As to read their rules for each place to Bs, without saying the names of the places. Bs must guess what the places are. Then Bs should read their rules to As.

....

Comment You can put the school rules on the walls around the classroom.

63

29 Describing actions 1

LANGUAGE	Present continuous.
TECHNIQUE	Organizing texts: describing a picture. Creating texts: write and do.
MATERIALS	Picture of a living-room on a poster.
PREPARATION	Make the poster.
TIME GUIDE	60 minutes.

Lead-in

1 Ask the learners to close their eyes and imagine a room. Ask them to decide what furniture it contains. Then tell them that four people are in the room. Ask them 'Who are they? What are they doing?' Give them a little time to imagine, then tell them to open their eyes.

2 Put the learners in pairs and get them to tell their partners what they 'saw'.

Organizing texts: describing a picture

3 Put up this picture:

Point to each person in the picture and ask the learners what he or she is doing. Supply any necessary vocabulary.

4 Tell the learners that they are going to write a description of the picture. Write the beginning of the description on the board:

Mrs Potter is sleeping in front of the television. But while she is peacefully sleeping, terrible things are happening all around her.

Encourage them to connect sentences with 'and' or 'while'.

Creating texts: write and do

5 Put the learners in groups of about eight. Ask each group to imagine that they are all members of the same family. Tell them to decide who is who, for example, grandmother, grandfather, aunt, uncle, mother, father, son, daughter.

6 Ask the groups to imagine a kitchen or living-room scene. Each person should imagine what they are doing. When you have given them a little time, ask the groups in turn to get up and form a tableau (they form a 'picture' by standing in their position in the room as if they are doing their action).

7 When all the groups have formed their tableaux, get them to prepare a description of the room and what everyone is doing in it. Each group should appoint a 'secretary' to write down the description.

8 Collect the descriptions and redistribute them so that each group now has another group's description. Each group should read the description it has been given, and form a tableau from it.

9 Ask the groups in turn to get up and form their tableau. The other groups should call out when they recognize their descriptions from these new tableaux.

30 Describing actions 2

LANGUAGE   Present continuous.

In the background; in the foreground.
On the left; on the right.
Behind; in front of; near.

TECHNIQUES   Organizing texts: describing a picture.
Creating texts: write and draw.

MATERIALS   Poster of a park scene; two pieces of paper for each learner.

PREPARATION   Make the poster.

TIME GUIDE   50 minutes.

Lead-in

1 Ask the learners to imagine the street outside the school. What are people doing there? Collect suggestions from the class.

Organizing texts: describing a picture

2 Put up this picture:

BALLOON RACE

Ask for volunteers to tell you some of the things that are happening in the picture.

3 Divide the class into three groups, as near the same size as possible. Ask the first group to write a description of the scene, starting on the left and describing it from left to right. Ask the second group to write a description, starting with the foreground and moving backwards. Ask the third group to write a description, starting with the background and moving forwards. Each group should appoint a 'secretary' to write their description.

4 Write some useful expressions on the board:

in the background
in the foreground
on the left
on the right
behind
in front of
near

5 Ask for a volunteer from each of the three groups to read out their descriptions to the rest of the class. Ask the class 'Which was the best way of organizing the description?' (In this picture, it is best to begin with the background to set the scene, and then to move forwards, finishing with the main event—the balloon race in the foreground.)

Creating texts: write and draw

6 Ask the learners to close their eyes and imagine a busy street. Then ask them to open their eyes and draw the picture they imagined.

7 Then ask them to write descriptions of the pictures they have drawn on a separate piece of paper.

8 Choose eight of the learners' descriptions and pictures. Separate the descriptions from the pictures. Label the descriptions A, B, C, etc. and label the pictures 1, 2, 3, etc. Take care that matching pictures and descriptions are not given corresponding letters and numbers (for example, make A some number other than 1, and C some number other than 3). Keep a list of the matching letters and numbers for yourself.

9 Put up the descriptions and pictures around the classroom, and ask the learners to read the descriptions and try to find the matching pictures.